LAND and WATER

Lake Michigan

by Anne Ylvisaker

Consultant:
Rosanne W. Fortner, Professor of Natural Resources
and Associate Director, F. T. Stone Laboratory
The Ohio State University
School of Natural Resources
Columbus, Ohio

Capstone press

Mankato, Minnesota

Fact Finders is published by Capstone Press
151 Good Counsel Drive, P.O. Box 669, Mankato, Minnesota 56002
http://www.capstone-press.com

Library of Congress Cataloging-in-Publication Data
Ylvisaker, Anne.
    Lake Michigan / by Anne Ylvisaker.
    v. cm. —(Fact finders. Land and water)
    Includes bibliographical references (p. 31) and index.
    Contents: Lake Michigan—Lake beginnings—Early people—American Indians and
settlers—Problems—Lake Michigan today.
    ISBN 0-7368-2210-0 (hardcover)
    1. Michigan, Lake—Juvenile literature. [1. Michigan, Lake.] I. Title. II. Series.

F553.Y588 2004
977.4—dc21   2003000325

Editorial Credits
Erika L. Shores, editor; Juliette Peters, designer and illustrator; Alta Schaffer,
    photo researcher; Eric Kudalis, product planning editor

Photo Credits
Cover image: Lake Michigan with Chicago skyline in background, Hisham F. Ibrahim/
    PhotoDisc/Getty Images

AP/Wide World Photos/Stephen J. Carrera, 22–23
Great Lakes Fishery Commission, 21 (both)
Houserstock/Jan Butchofsky, 24–25, 27
The Image Finders/William Manning, 1
Library of Congress, 4–5
North Wind Picture Archives, 14–15, 17, 18–19
Root Resources/Leonard Gordon, 26
Stock Montage Inc./The Newberry Library, 12–13
Visuals Unlimited/Pat Anderson, 10; Ross Frid, 11

1 2 3 4 5 6 08 07 06 05 04 03

Table of Contents

Chapter 1

Lake Michigan

One of the worst ship disasters in Lake Michigan's history happened before the ship left port. The *Eastland* was docked in Chicago on July 24, 1915. Most of the 2,500 passengers on board were going on vacation. A tugboat started to pull the ship out of the harbor. But the ship was still tied to the dock.

As the tugboat pulled, the ship leaned but did not move forward. Scared passengers ran to the leaning side to see what was happening. Their weight tilted the boat even farther. The leaning ship tossed passengers into the water. They fell on top of one another. More than 800 people died.

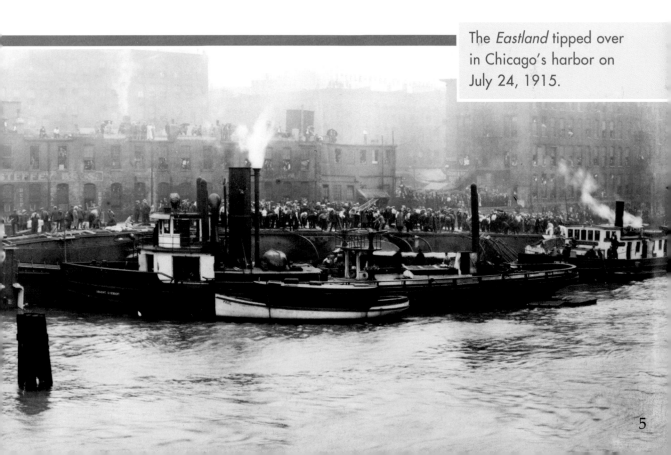

The *Eastland* tipped over in Chicago's harbor on July 24, 1915.

The Great Lakes

Lakes Superior, Huron, Michigan, Ontario, and Erie are the Great Lakes of North America. Lake Michigan is the only Great Lake that lies completely within the United States. Wisconsin, Michigan, Illinois, and Indiana surround Lake Michigan.

Straits, rivers, and canals join the Great Lakes to each other and to the Atlantic Ocean. Together, the Great Lakes and the waterways connecting them make up the St. Lawrence Seaway.

Lake Michigan is the sixth largest lake in the world. It is 307 miles (494 kilometers) long and 118 miles (190 kilometers) wide. The average depth of the lake is 279 feet (85 meters). The deepest part is 923 feet (281 meters).

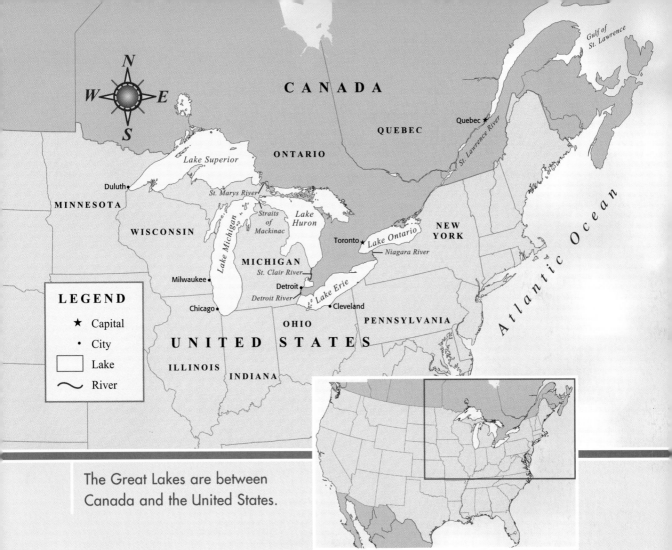

The Great Lakes are between Canada and the United States.

St. Lawrence Seaway

The St. Lawrence Seaway opened in 1959. Ships could bring goods from Europe and other places by traveling through the Great Lakes and its waterways. The seaway turned some cities on the Great Lakes into busy shipping ports.

Chapter 2

Lake Beginnings

Thousands of years ago, glaciers covered the Great Lakes area. These huge, slow-moving sheets of ice pressed down the land. Glaciers also moved rocks that scraped the earth. The pressure and scraping carved wide valleys. Over time, the glaciers melted. The Great Lakes formed when water filled the valleys.

The shape of the lakes changed over thousands of years. Long ago, Lake Michigan and Lake Huron were not joined. Today, the Straits of Mackinac join the two lakes.

MICHIGAN
Upper Peninsula

Straits of Mackinac

Lake Huron

Green Bay

Grand Traverse Bay

Traverse City •

Green Bay •

Lake Michigan

MICHIGAN
Lower Peninsula

WISCONSIN

Milwaukee •

LEGEND
• City
▭ Lake

ILLINOIS

Chicago •

• Gary

INDIANA

UNITED STATES

Thick forests grow on Lake Michigan's northern and western shores.

Lake Michigan splits the state of Michigan into two parts. They are the Upper Peninsula and the Lower Peninsula. The Upper Peninsula has more hills and lakes than the Lower Peninsula.

The land near Lake Michigan is varied. Forests cover areas north and west of the lake. Sand dunes lie along the eastern and southern shores. Wind and waves push sand into these large piles. The dunes always change. Over hundreds of years, sand blocked some rivers into the lake. The blocked rivers then turned into lakes.

Sleeping Bear Dunes

Sleeping Bear Dunes are found in Traverse Bay. They are the highest sand dunes in the world. Visitors can climb the dunes at Sleeping Bear Dunes National Lakeshore.

Chapter 3

Early People

The Ottawa, Ojibwa, and Potawatomi Indians were the first people to live near Lake Michigan. They lived in dome-shaped homes called wigwams. They fished and hunted. They gathered wild rice. They used sap from maple trees to make sugar.

Frenchman Samuel de Champlain was the first European to explore the Great Lakes. In the 1600s, he sent Frenchman Jean Nicolet to live among the American Indians. The French wanted to make friends with the Indians in order to trade with them.

Long ago, Ojibwa Indians
gathered wild rice in canoes.

Nicolet met Indian tribes living
in the area that is now Green
Bay, Wisconsin. In 1634, Nicolet
traveled in a canoe through the
Ottawa River, Lake Nipissing, and

the French River. He reached Lake Huron. He then went through the Straits of Mackinac and into Lake Michigan.

In 1673, explorers Louis Jolliet and Jacques Marquette explored the Fox River. This river flows from Lake Michigan to the Mississippi River. The explorers thought the river would take them west. Instead, they discovered that the Mississippi River leads to the Gulf of Mexico.

Jean Nicolet (right) met with American Indians living in what is now Wisconsin.

Chapter 4

American Indians and Settlers

American Indians near Lake Michigan hunted beaver, elk, deer, bear, and many other animals. They traded the animal skins to Europeans and Americans at fur trading posts. In return, they received guns, pots, sugar, and other goods.

The fur trade changed the American Indians' way of life. Before the fur trade, they hunted only what they needed. They made their own tools and grew their own food. During the fur trade, American Indians spent most of their time catching animals and preparing the hides for trade.

American Indians hunted deer and other animals.
The Indians traded furs for guns, pots, and sugar.

Over time, the number of animals in the area decreased. American Indians could no longer find enough furs to trade. Without the fur trade, settlers living near Lake Michigan needed a new way to

make money. Forests growing along Lake Michigan gave them the chance they needed. Trees were cut down and turned into lumber. People used lumber to build homes, buildings, and ships. Cities grew as more people came to work in the lumber business.

The end of the fur trade changed the American Indians' way of life again. Settlers now wanted the American Indians' land for lumber and farming. Settlers made laws that forced American Indians off the land. Reservations were set aside for American Indians. The U.S. government forced Americans Indians to move to these areas or find other places to live.

Chicago, Illinois, became an important city on Lake Michigan during the 1800s.

Chapter 5

Problems

People have fished in Lake Michigan for many years. Whitefish, sturgeon, and trout are some of the fish living in the lake. Some people sell the fish they catch.

In the 1930s, sea lampreys found their way into Lake Michigan. Lampreys are jawless fish with snakelike bodies. They attach to fish, suck their blood, and kill them.

Within 20 years, fish important to Lake Michigan nearly disappeared. Dead fish floated on Lake Michigan. People often caught fish that had big scars from the lamprey's bite.

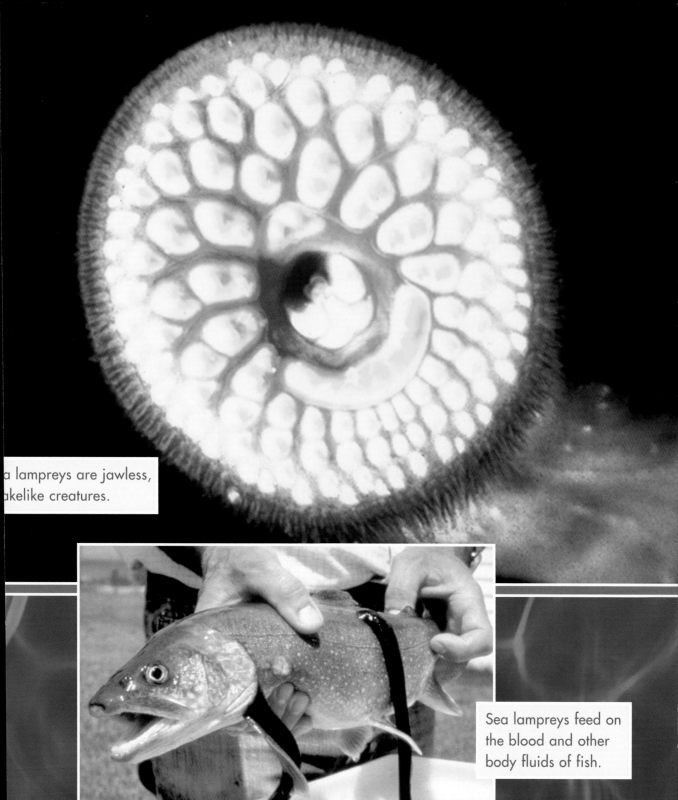

a lampreys are jawless,
akelike creatures.

Sea lampreys feed on
the blood and other
body fluids of fish.

Scientists from the United States and Canada worked to solve the problem. They blocked streams where lampreys were born. The scientists treated the streams with chemicals that killed lampreys. The scientists' work paid off. The number of fish in Lake Michigan has gone up in recent years.

Today, Lake Michigan's fish are not harmed by sea lampreys. But other animals and plants are entering the lake. These animals and plants are not native to the Great Lakes area. Scientists are watching to see how the animals and plants might change Lake Michigan.

Electric fish barriers are placed in some rivers. The barriers keep sea lampreys from entering Lake Michigan.

Chapter 6

Lake Michigan Today

Today, Lake Michigan and its ports play an important role in the Great Lakes' shipping industry. Southern ports ship steel from Indiana and Michigan. Steel is used to make building materials, railroads, cars, and many other products.

Nearly 12 million people live in the areas around Lake Michigan. Chicago, Milwaukee, and the city of Gary, Indiana, are large cities along the lake.

Skyscrapers line the shores of Lake Michigan in Chicago, Illinois.

Tourism is important to Lake Michigan. In summer, people fish, sail, and water ski on the lake. Tourists enjoy the sandy beaches lining Lake Michigan's shore.

People living near Lake Michigan know the lake is important. They work to keep the lake clean and healthy. People want to enjoy Lake Michigan for many years to come.

Colorful boats sail on Lake Michigan during summer.

People come to Lake Michigan's beaches to play in the sand and go swimming.

Fast Facts

Length: 307 miles (494 kilometers)

Width: 118 miles (190 kilometers)

Average depth: 279 feet (85 meters)

Maximum depth: 923 feet (281 meters)

Shoreline length: 1,640 miles (2,639 kilometers)

Population surrounding the lake: 12 million

Weather: Lake Michigan's eastern shores have warm summers and mild winters. The western shores have cold winters and warm summers. The southern part of the lake does not freeze in the winter.

Fish: Lake Michigan has more than 100 kinds of fish. Some of these fish are lake sturgeon, brook trout, northern pike, lake herring, walleye, and rock bass.

Hands On: Sea Lamprey Tag

Sea lampreys entered the Great Lakes in the 1930s. Sea lampreys killed or harmed many fish in Lake Michigan. Some fish moved into other lakes to escape the sea lamprey. You can play this game with your friends and pretend to be fish and sea lampreys.

What You Need

Chalk
Large group of friends
Paved outdoor area

What You Do

1. Draw five large circles on the ground. The circles should be large enough for 4 or more players to stand in. The circles are the Great Lakes.
2. Choose one player to be the sea lamprey.
3. The rest of the players should split up and stand in four of the lakes. Leave one lake empty. These players are the fish.
4. The sea lamprey stands outside the circles. The game begins when the sea lamprey chooses a lake to "invade." The sea lamprey enters a circle and tries to tag as many fish as he or she can. Players must run to the empty lake without being tagged. These fish are safe. A tagged fish is out of the game.
5. The sea lamprey moves to the next lake when all the fish in the first lake are tagged or safe. The fish in the second lake must move to the empty lake to be safe.
6. The game continues until all the fish are safe or tagged out. The sea lamprey then counts how many fish he or she tagged out. Repeat the game with a different player as the sea lamprey. See which players can catch the most fish.

Glossary

disaster (duh-ZASS-tur)—an event that causes a great deal of damage or suffering

dune (DOON)—a sand hill made by the wind; dunes can form near oceans or large lakes or in a desert

glacier (GLAY-shur)—a large, slow-moving sheet of ice and snow

industry (IN-duh-stree)—businesses that make products or provide services

native (NAY-tiv)—belonging to an area

port (PORT)—a harbor or place where boats and ships can dock or anchor safely

strait (STRAYT)—a narrow strip of water that connects two larger bodies of water

Internet Sites

Do you want to find out more about Lake Michigan?
Let FactHound, our fact-finding hound dog, do the research for you.

Here's how:
1) Visit *http://www.facthound.com*
2) Type in the **BOOK ID** number: **0736822100**
3) Click on **FETCH IT.**

FactHound will fetch Internet sites picked by our editors just for you!

Read More

Beckett, Harry. *Lake Michigan.* Great Lakes of North America. Vero Beach, Fla.: Rourke, 1999.

Gibson, Karen Bush. *The Potawatomi.* Native Peoples. Mankato, Minn.: Bridgestone Books, 2003.

Todd, Anne M. *The Ojibwa: People of the Great Lakes.* American Indian Nations. Mankato, Minn.: Bridgestone Books, 2003.

Index ——————

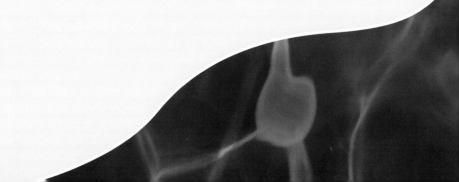